Praise for the Option Method

"I know I will keep using this method probably for a long time to come, if not forever! I am indebted to Bruce as well as you Deborah, for continuing to spread his legacy. It's sheer GENIUS!"
— Jan Frijters, The Netherlands

"I have been doing dialogues with myself, and have had some quite startling realizations. It is clearly a very powerful tool!"
— Randy Austill

"You likely won't be surprised to hear that reading Bruce's book was one of the most profound experiences of my life. I got through 30 pages the first night, had intense and 'insightful' dreams and awoke to a transformed world."
— Sue Kranz

"The Option idea is a very powerful one and it has had a strong impact on my life."
— John McIlroy

"I was immediately stunned by the technique. It seems to not only meet all my 'ideal' criteria — simple, fast, elegant, respectful, easy, fun, and powerful — but exceeds what I thought was possible . . . and that's after using it only twice! I remain as dazzled as ever by the simple but extraordinary power and elegance of the questions."
— Vincent O'Kelly, United Kingdom

"I was so amazed to learn about this method and how easy it can be to become happy."
— Lutz Stradmann, Germany

"Your late husband and you have given the world a GREAT gift."
— Bob Marino

"I had so much energy after our talk that I went out for a long walk, processing so much. It felt like such an answer for me that I have been searching for for quite sometime now. This morning I felt newly encouraged to do my own dialogue around a struggle I've had for a long time with my spiritual journey . . . I was able to get to a whole new place."
— Judy White

"I ran across the Option Method about a year before I actually experienced it and recognized some of the truth in it but not to the degree that I do now. Now it has become a way of life as well as a philosophy of how to help people. It has made a world of difference in my life."
— Richard Banton

"After my last couple of dialogues I reached a point of inner contentment, peace and happiness with being right where I am. It's a great feeling. Something I have always wanted to experience."
— Rae Foster

Also by Bruce Di Marsico and Deborah Mendel

The Key to a Happy Life
Bruce Di Marsico Presents the Option Method
(Audio CD)

The Happiness Secret: Is Happiness a Choice?
The Option Method Philosophy
(Two Audio CD Set)

Unlock Your Happiness With Five Simple Questions:
The Option Method
by Bruce M. Di Marsico

Be Happier Now
Your Personal Roadmap
to a Life of Joy and Happiness

The Option Method Workbook

Deborah Mendel

Dragonfly Press

Copyright © 2006 Deborah Mendel

Published by Dragonfly Press
C/O Deborah Mendel
P.O. Box 1192
Walnut Grove, CA 95690

Illustrations and Cover Art: Chris Spencer

Portrait of Bruce Di Marsico by Bruce Hancock

ISBN: 978-0-9704795-3-2

Be Happier Now — Your Personal Roadmap to a Life of Joy and Happiness: The Option Method Workbook.

First Edition

Printed and bound in the United States of America by
Morris Publishing • *www.morrispublishing.com* • 800-650-7888

1 2 3 4 5 6 7 8 9 10

To my dear Bruce,
still touching our lives,
still helping so many —
your legacy lives on.

"... Unhappiness happens in the dark, it happens in the half light of reason. The problem is that you think you know that you have to be unhappy. I suggest that it's questionable. What if what you are feeling is just the result of a belief you have?"

— Bruce Di Marsico

What is the Option Method?

The Option Method is a unique yet simple self-help tool designed to help you become happier. The way the Option Method works is that it helps you to uncover the beliefs that are behind your bad feelings. By using the Option Method Questions you will reveal to yourself what beliefs you have been holding onto, what mythical beliefs you have had that have been obstructing your path to happiness. They may be subtle or obvious. The Option Method will help you realize why you have not been happy or why you are continually upset about some things in your life.

Where did the Option Method come from?

The Option Method was created by Bruce Di Marsico in the early 1970's. Bruce realized that people were unhappy, sad, angry and all other negative emotions because they in some way believed that they had to be. They believed that they had no choice. He designed his Option Method Questions to help reveal to the suffering person that they could feel better, that they had a choice. It is through the use of the Option Method Questions that we can discover in a real practical way what role our beliefs play in our emotional state and feeling of well being. When we are free from these self-defeating and mythical beliefs, we find ourselves naturally happier in life.

What is the purpose of this workbook?

This workbook will help you master the use of Option Method to help yourself become the person you want to be. You define what that is. Do you want to be less frustrated? Do you wish you could stop being angry with your loved ones when they disappoint you? Do you realize that you take things too personally and don't know how to stop? Do you wish you could stop feeling so lonely? Do you wish you could achieve more in life, that you have a sense you are holding yourself back? Do you fear being rejected? Do you simply wish you could feel free to be yourself? Do you want to be happier? This workbook will show you how to use the Option Method and apply it in real life situations that seem to give you emotional challenges.

How do I begin to learn and practice the Option Method for myself?

You may begin right here with this workbook alone or you may want to familiarize yourself with the work of the creator of the Option Method, Bruce Di Marsico before you begin. Reading his written material and listening to his audio lectures will give you a basic understanding of the Option Method philosophy and the questions as Bruce taught it. Doing so will lay the groundwork for your personal explorations in using the Option Method Questions for yourself. It will give you a sense of what the Option Method is all about, who Bruce was, and the whole attitude and approach of the method he created to help us unravel our unhappiness.

What do I need to know in order to practice the Option Method?

There is nothing you need to know except yourself. You will be asked to be honest with yourself. You will want to be patient with yourself. Don't demand of yourself immediate "ah ha's!" Expect to be occasionally dumbstruck. This is the beginning of learning and changing. You have been going through life with many assumptions and beliefs, some since childhood that have never been challenged or exposed before. The Option Method Questions will shed light on them giving you the opportunity to disown them and let them go.

When can I use the Option Method?

You can use the Option Method anytime. If you become aware that you are feeling a way you don't like you can use the Option Method Questions to see if it is *really* necessary. As you become more adept at using the questions you will move more quickly through them to get to the heart of the matter. The more you use them the more you will begin to understand yourself and what your reasons are for feeling bad. The mystery of the source of your distresses will dissipate. You will understand in time how your beliefs have been affecting your emotions.

Let's get started!

"When you are unhappy it is because you believe you should be. You feel it is necessary. Whenever you are unhappy (or angry, sad, frightened; use your own words) you can become happy by asking yourself: "If it were possible, would I like to be happy and suffer less?" If your answer is YES, then ask yourself these [Option Method] questions."

— Bruce Di Marsico

The Option Method Questions

* *What* am I unhappy about? (Identify)
* What do I mean? (Clarify)
* *What* [is it] *about that*, that makes me unhappy? (Identify)
* What do I mean? (Clarify)
* *Why* am I unhappy about that?
* What do I mean? (Clarify)
* *What am I afraid it would mean* if I were not unhappy about that? or
  What am I afraid would happen if I were not unhappy about that?
* *Why would it* have to *mean that*?
* *Do I still believe* that [being happy would be bad for me right now]?

These are the Option Method Questions. Remember that when using these questions you will substitute the word "unhappy" for whatever bad feeling you are having right now. It may be sad, angry, worried or perhaps frightened. The point is you must put your feelings into your own words. The word "unhappy" is used here simply as a generalized term to describe a negative way of feeling for the purpose of outlining the Option Method Questions. It is important that you use your own words to describe your feelings and emotions. If the word *unhappy* best describes how you feel then go ahead and use that word.

The purpose of the first two Option Method Questions are to help you identify and clarify exactly *what* is bothering you. The third question will help you to begin to reveal what belief is behind what is bothering you, the *why* of the matter. The fourth question helps you narrow it down to the core belief that is holding you back from feeling better, the thing you are *afraid it would mean* or what you are *afraid would happen* should you go ahead and feel better right now. Finally, the fifth and sixth questions give you the opportunity to now question that belief; *would it* [*have to*] *mean that*?

This workbook will guide you through the process of asking yourself the Option Method Questions. Blank pages have been provided in this book so that you may write down your answers to each of the questions. You may of course use your own blank book if you find this more to your liking. These questions will help you to open the door to your heart. Those beliefs you've acquired that have been obstructing your path to a happier life will fall away. Your true feelings will become evident. It's easy and painless, because it's about knowing who you really are. There is nothing to memorize or study. You are your own best expert. To begin you must first identify your initial bad feeling, asking yourself the first Option Method Question will help you do this.

The First Option Method Question

What am I unhappy about?

   Personalize this question. Substitute the word *unhappy* in this question for one that best express-es the bad feeling you have that you would like to change. For instance, you may be feeling worried about something. If so, you would ask yourself, "What am I <u>worried</u> about?" Clarify your answer. Narrow it down. If, for example, your initial answer to this question is something like, "I'm <u>worried</u> about my <u>health</u>," that is a very broad answer. This is a great place to start but narrow it down and be as specific as possible. Ask yourself **"What do I mean?"** This will help you clarify your answer to the first question.

The First Option Method Question

What am I _____ about? (Identify)

The First Option Method Question

What am I _____ about? (Identify)

What do I mean? (Clarify)

As you clarify your answer you may have found that you have changed your description of what you are upset about or maybe not. Either way asking yourself the first Option Method Question again will only help you to more clearly identify what is bothering you the most at this time.

The First Option Method Question

What am I _____ about? (Identify)

The First Option Method Question

What am I _____ about? (Identify)

What do I mean? (Clarify)

When you feel satisfied that you have answered the first question as best as you can move on to the second Option Method Question. This second question will help you to clarify even further what is bothering you.

The Second Option Method Question

What is it *about that*, that makes me unhappy?

Using our previous example about worrying, you would ask yourself, "What is it about my <u>health</u> that makes me <u>worried</u>?" or "What is it about my <u>health</u> that I am <u>worried</u> about?" Use your own answers to the first question and fill in the blanks of the second question. We are still trying to clarify more specifically what you feel bad about. By asking yourself *"what about it?"* [bothers, frightens, saddens, angers you] you will get all the more closer to recognizing the fundamental basis for your bad feelings. Again, asking yourself "What do I mean?" following this question will help you to clarify your answer.

The Second Option Method Question

What is it *about* _____ , *that* makes me _____ ? (Identify)

The Second Option Method Question

What is it *about* _____ , *that* makes me _____ ? (Identify)

What do I mean? (Clarify)

The Second Option Method Question

What is it *about that*, that makes me unhappy?

Let's look at what you have identified and understand more clearly this second question. You have begun to zero in on your beliefs with your initial response to the second question. Now it is time to narrow it down even further. In fact, if you look closely at your answer it is most likely that you have simply restated in another way *what* you are feeling badly about, but the second question is asking you to clarify *what about that* bothers you. Imagine that you are beginning to peel back the many layers of an onion, getting closer and closer to its core. It is this core or core belief, which is underlying your negative feelings. This is what your goal is, to get to that core. Take your time. You have never looked at your thoughts quite this way before.

Let's use our example again and create a sample dialogue to show you how this second question works:

Question: *"What is it about my <u>health</u> that makes me <u>worried</u>?"*

Answer: *"I know that I don't take very good care of my health."*

Q: *"What do I mean?" (clarify)*

A: *"Well, I know I don't eat the right foods, I don't exercise enough, and I'm gaining weight."*

Q: *"What is it about your not eating the right foods, exercising enough and gaining weight that worries you?"*

A: *"It's going to catch up with me eventually. Like my father, I could have a heart attack if I don't change my ways."*

Q: *"What is it about its catching up with you that worries you?"*

A: *"I'm <u>afraid I might have a heart attack</u> like my father did."*

In this example you will notice that although we began with a worry about health, when we continued to explore and clarify what we are worried about we find we are actually ". . . afraid I might have a heart attack . . ." In our example we have arrived at a more specific answer by asking the second question again and clarifying what we mean. Try using the second question again to get closer to that which is bothering you the most and only then move on to the third question.

The Second Option Method Question

What is it *about* _____ , *that* makes me _____ ? (Identify)

The Second Option Method Question

What is it *about* _____ , *that* makes me _____ ? (Identify)

What do I mean? (Clarify)

The Third Option Method Question

Why am I unhappy about that?

   Let's examine and understand what this question means and why are we asking *why*. "Why" means *for what reason of mine?* This is one of the most important questions you may ever ask yourself. This question prompts you to recognize that you have your own very personal reasons for feeling the way you feel. Often we get so caught up in our emotions that we have completely forgotten we are not actually feeling this way against our will. We no longer "feel like" we have a choice or an option to feel differently but this is an illusion. The bad feeling you are experiencing now follows from a belief. As you ask yourself *why*, when looking at *your* reason, you will reveal your belief. This wonderful, simple question gives you a renewed opportunity to begin your own self-enlightenment. When you ask this question you may at first answer "I always have been" or "wouldn't anyone?" Rephrase the question to mean "What is *my* reason now for being unhappy about it?"

   Let's apply this question to our example. If you remember, the last response in our example was "I'm afraid I might have a heart attack like my father did." To use the third question we would ask "Why am I afraid I might have a heart attack like my father?" Let's try it out, remembering that *why* means: For what reason of mine?

Question: *"Why am I afraid I might have a heart attack like my father?"*

Answer: *"Well, everybody's afraid of heart attacks!"*

Q: *"But why am I afraid of having a heart attack like my father, what is my reason?"*

A: *"Well, when my father had his heart attack he had to quit his job. It was a real hardship on our family. My mother had to support us and I had to get a part time job in order to help out. My father was miserable and it was just downhill from there. I have a family to support too . . . God, I'd hate to do that to my family. I would really be letting them down. I don't want to do that to them. I could never forgive myself."*

The Third Option Method Question

Why am I unhappy about that?

Do you understand how we have used this question to get very specific? We have now arrived at just what it is about not taking care of our health that is worrying us. "I would really be letting them down." In our example we have revealed that we are afraid of not supporting our family in the future and "letting them down." There could be other reasons for another person. For instance, if you had no family to support you could be afraid of becoming dependant on strangers, of being lonely and ill. Perhaps you might fear being rejected as a diseased person. There are as many reasons as there are people.

Once you have identified your own personal reason for feeling bad you will move on to the next questions. Review and summarize your answers. You may have found that what you were initially upset or unhappy about has seemingly evolved into something else. Write down now what best describes your feelings at this point and answer the questions as succinctly as possible. Collect your thoughts. Referring back to your previous answers may be helpful. Remember that this is your path and there can be no wrong turns. You are your own best expert.

Review & Summarize

What am I _____ about?

What is it *about* _____ , *that* makes me _____ ?

The Third Option Method Question

Why am I _____ about that? (Identify)
(What is *my* reason?)

The Third Option Method Question

Why am I _____ about that? (Identify)
(What is *my* reason?)

What do I mean? (Clarify)

    Has your answer changed somewhat now that you have considered your reason? Have you perhaps put new words to your feelings? Ask yourself *why* again, this time with your new clarified response. Chances are you have never asked yourself this question before. Be patient with yourself and remember that *your* reason is the only one that counts.

The Third Option Method Question

Why am I _____ about that? (Identify)
(What is *my* reason?)

The Third Option Method Question

Why am I _____ about that? (Identify)
(What is *my* reason?)

What do I mean? (Clarify)

Event – Belief – Response

When you ask yourself why you are unhappy about something, you are revealing your *beliefs*. The Option Method is specifically designed to shed light on these beliefs. Bruce Di Marsico taught that when something happens, an event in our lives, we have a belief about it. Our response to that belief is a feeling. Sometimes the event is only imagined; it has not even happened yet but we anticipate that it will. There are three fundamental beliefs that affect our feelings or response. If we believe that the event is bad for our happiness we can't help but feel bad or unhappy. If we believe that the event is good for our happiness then we will feel good. If we believe it will be neither good nor bad for our happiness we will feel more neutral or okay with it.

Consider this scenario: You are in an intimate relationship with someone. You are happy together; you are both enjoying each other and the time you spend together. One day you have a disagreement. It turns into a fight. You both decide to break-up. Your emotional responses however to the identical event, the break-up of your relationship, are completely different and you will each feel very differently about it. Your judgments and beliefs about the event will directly affect how each of you will feel about the break-up.

Your former partner may feel relieved, almost happy. They have been thinking that perhaps the relationship was not exactly what they wanted but did not know how to end it. They walk away feeling: "I'll be better off out of this relationship." They feel better and are looking forward to finding the right person for them.

You, on the other hand, may feel very unhappy. You may be feeling (believing) that you can't imagine how you can be happy and feel fulfilled without this person and the connection you had with them. Your response may be something like: "How can I be happy without them?"

Both of you have very different beliefs about what has happened and your future happiness. Your feelings to the same event will reflect this.

An Event —   *The ending of a close relationship*

Belief —   *This is good for me that the relationship is over*
                        This is bad for me that the relationship is over
                        This is neither good nor bad that the relationship is over

Emotional   *Feeling relieved and happy that the relationship is over*
Response —   *Feeling unhappy that the relationship is over*
                        Feeling okay that the relationship is over

The Fourth Option Method Question

What am I afraid it would mean if I were not unhappy about that? Or

What am I afraid would happen if I were not unhappy about that?

At this point you have identified *why* you have been unhappy or feeling bad. You have clarified your reasons and made them very specific and personal. Clearly, up until this point, you have felt that you have a good reason to feel the way you have been feeling. Or you have perhaps felt that you had no choice but to feel bad in this situation or that. The fourth Option Method Question will give you the chance to consider the possibility of not feeling the way you have been feeling. Since you have brought yourself to a specific issue you will be able to apply this question very directly to it. This question will help you to uncover the belief you have had that keeps you from feeling better. Nothing is actually forcing you to feel bad, to feel a way you really don't like to feel. You have been believing that to not feel bad right now would be worse. Let's look at what would be worse. What would be so bad about feeling okay right now?

Before I demonstrate with our example I want you to try using the fourth question for yourself. Again, fill in the blanks with your answer. You may need to rephrase the tail end of this question to suit your answer from the third question. The important part of this question is *"What am I afraid would happen or what am I afraid it would mean if . . . ?"* As in our example *"What am I afraid would happen if I were not feeling afraid of letting my family down?"*

This question is not meant to imply that you should be feeling differently. This question will help you see just why you have been resisting feeling better up until now. You have had an unspoken and unrecognized belief that has been preventing you from feeling better. You can't help but do and feel what you believe is in your own best interest. It has been literally unthinkable up until this point to even imagine feeling better. Imagine now that you have stopped feeling those bad feelings, whatever they are. *What are you afraid it would mean* or *what are you afraid might happen?* Use either form of this question. Use whatever question you best relate to at this time. Your answer may not make sense to you. Just answer the question honestly. Imagine yourself not being unhappy given the situation that you're feeling bad about. Try saying your answer out loud, this often helps and write down your answer.

If you find that you simply can't answer this question, but you still don't feel better, go back to clarifying *what* it is that you are unhappy about by asking yourself the first Option Method Question again. You cannot get lost on your own path to greater happiness.

The Fourth Option Method Question

What am I afraid would happen if I were not _____ about that?

What am I afraid it would mean if I were not _____ about that?

The Fourth Option Method Question

What am I afraid would happen if I were not _____ about that?

What am I afraid it would mean if I were not _____ about that?

What do I mean? (Clarify)

The Fourth Option Method Question

What am I afraid would happen if I were not _____ *about that?*
What am I afraid it would mean if I were not _____ *about that?*

Using our example we would ask the following:

Question: *"**What am I afraid would happen** if I were not feeling afraid of letting my family down?"*

Answer: *"I don't want to do that to them! I love them. I want to take care of them!"*

Q: *"Yes, of course I want to take care of them, of course I love them, but **what am I afraid it would mean** if I stopped being afraid of letting down my family?"*

A: *"How could I stop being afraid of letting them down? I mean I really care about them. That would be like not caring."*

What belief has been revealed in the answer above? Was it similar to your own answer to the fourth question? Look at the final statement in our example. "That would be like not caring." I have found that in the more than three decades that I have been studying and using the Option Method for myself and with others, that this is a very common belief. People believe that if they were not unhappy in a given situation that it would mean that they did not care about what they *do* care about. Another way that this is often expressed is that if they stopped being upset they would just not bother to try to get what they wanted. They would become apathetic. The truth is they do care and it does matter to them. Sometimes we're afraid that another person will interpret our not being upset as the same as not caring.

Before I go on to guide you through this next question, I would like to share with you a very real life example of how I used the Method myself while in the middle of writing this workbook. I believe you may find it helpful.

My companion/partner was out of town traveling to an exotic island with another friend. We would be out of contact for over a week. It was a perfect time to write as it gave me time to have total focus on this project. But as the days wore on I began to think about his absence and the events surrounding his departure. Each day since his departure some one would cross my path and either ask about him or mention their own plans they had made with their spouses or companions for travel together. I was not missing him but I was beginning to feel rather left out and disappointed that I had not gone with him. Each time a friend innocently brought up the subject of traveling and companionship it was as if a seed of discontentment was being planted in my spirit. I initially dropped my thoughts of regrets and disappointments and let them pass, knowing that this trip was important to him and there would be time enough for us to do things together when he returned.

What was remarkable was how every day someone said something to me that brought me back to these unpleasant thoughts. I was building a case, a very strong case, for me to be upset, unhappy and disappointed. I began to have trouble sleeping and watched myself in amazement. Was I really doing this and why wasn't I stopping? I sat in front of the computer one day working on this workbook and my thoughts wandered to him on his "tropical paradise trip." I was now imagining him having the most wonderful time of his life without me! I was hurt and furious! The irony of the situation was not lost on me either. Here I was writing a step by step guide on how to use the Option Method and I was getting terribly upset myself. I was now in tears. I had not been this unhappy about anything in years and I wondered aloud "What are you doing?"

I looked back at my work on the computer and decided it was time to use the workbook for myself. "Well, let's see if this workbook works!" I began with the first question and treated myself as if I had never used the Option Method before. I grabbed a legal pad and began by writing the questions down along with my answers. By now I was in tears but was determined to give this workbook a real test and most of all feel better! Here is what I wrote:

Question: *What am I so upset about?*

Answer: *I'm upset because he's gone away without me.*

Q: *What is it about his going away without you that upsets you so?*

A: *I feel left out, rejected. Why didn't he want me with him? We always work together but never seem to find time to play together.*

Q: *What is there about your always working together but not finding time to play together that is upsetting you?*

A: *If we keep this up we will get bored with each other. We do have fun working together, but I want to play too. It's like we are in a rut.*

Q: *Why am I upset about us being in this rut?*

A: *If we continue this way our relationship will never grow. We will be stuck in this route behavior together, never sharing new experiences. Our relationship will grow stale and we will both tire of it. I want our relationship to grow and flourish. I'm realizing now that <u>we really need to change</u> what we've been doing. This isn't going to work.*

Q: *Okay, I know I strongly believe that we have to change what we have been doing or the relationship won't work. I want to change what we've been doing; I'm getting myself in a rut. **What am I afraid would happen** if I stopped being upset right now about our need to change and being in this rut?*

A: *This relationship is very important to me. If I let this issue be okay right now, if I stop feeling so upset about this, I'm afraid my other feelings will die too. I mean, what if my other feelings for him just fade away? I feel very passionate right now about this. If I calm down now I'm afraid the next thing to follow will be my other feelings for him. I'm afraid that my other feelings for him will die or become neutralized. I won't care about anything about us anymore. I don't want that to happen.*

At this point I put down the pad and pen. I was not ready to really finish the Option Method dialogue with myself. I had exhausted myself and I went to lie down and take a nap. I woke up later and looked down at what I had written. I couldn't believe what I read. *"I'm afraid that my other feelings for him will die or become neutralized."* I was not about to give up being upset when it meant that I might stop caring all together. It was time to ask myself the last Option Method Questions. In my case all I needed was to ask myself *"**Why would it have to mean that?**"* and I quickly realized that what I was believing was untrue. That if I stopped being upset right now about all of these issues I would not stop caring. In fact, I cared so much that I'd been putting myself through a lot of misery because I cared. I was not about to stop caring.

Bruce Di Marsico discovered that this is the most common reason why people get unhappy. He found in his decades of work with people who were unhappy, that we are usually unhappy because we believe that if we weren't we would be bad for ourselves somehow. We would be bad for what we wanted. In my case I would stop caring and that is the last thing that I wanted to do!

Ask yourself the fourth question again. Really consider this question. If you feel you can't answer it or it doesn't seem relevant, revisit the third question, *"**Why am I unhappy about that?**"* You may need to clarify your answer further before using the fourth question. I was able to move quickly through the questions for myself because I am very familiar with them. Your answers may take a little more time and you may need to write more down in order to make it clear to yourself. Often when we use the Option Method we find that what we thought we were unhappy about is not exactly what we are most unhappy about. We discover, by using these questions, the underlying fear or worry that was not quite so obvious before.

The Fourth Option Method Question

What am I afraid would happen if I were not _____ about that?

What am I afraid it would mean if I were not _____ about that?

The Fourth Option Method Question

What am I afraid would happen if I were not _____ about that?

What am I afraid it would mean if I were not _____ about that?

What do I mean? (Clarify)

The Option Method Questions
Review & Summarize

Reflect back on your answers to the Option Method Questions. Look back at your answers on the previous pages if this helps you to do so. Now summarize your responses to the questions as simply and succinctly as possible. Write your answers down on this worksheet and you will be ready to move on to the last questions. When you are satisfied with your summary it is time to approach the last Option Method Questions.

What am I unhappy about? (Identify)

What [is it] *about that*, that makes me unhappy? (Identify)

Why am I unhappy about that?

What am I afraid it would mean if I were not unhappy about that? *or*
What am I afraid would happen if I were not unhappy about that?

"Certain things were true for us when we were children that we had reasons for believing, that served a purpose, that helped us to be happy. As we became adults they no longer worked for us, they no longer helped us, they no longer served us and yet we continued to believe them. We no longer had a reason to believe them."

— Bruce M. Di Marsico

The Fifth and Sixth Option Method Questions

Why would it have to mean that [I don't care what I care about, for example]? *or*
Do I still believe that [being happy would be bad for me right now]?

This first question is actually a rhetorical one. This is why I have put these questions together. You don't really want to find a reason why you still have to feel bad and be unhappy. It is helpful though to hear this question and to consider it if only for the purpose of questioning your belief. The second question, "Do I still believe that?" is more of a direct challenge that will give you an opportunity to reconsider now what you have been believing and realize that you really don't believe it anymore.

Question 4 — *What am I afraid it would mean* if I were not unhappy about that? *or*
What am I afraid would happen if I were not unhappy about that?

Question 5 — *Why would it have to mean that?*

Question 6 — *Do I still believe that* [being happy would be bad for me right now]?

Let's look at these questions together now to appreciate why we are asking them and how they can help you change how you feel.

Question 4 helps you to realize that you are preferring and choosing to be unhappy because you are afraid that if you were happy it would mean you didn't care about what you see yourself as caring about.

Questions 5 & 6 will help you recognize that even if you were happy now, you are still for whatever you are for and against whatever you are against. Being happy is not contradictory to your values or desires.

Once you have asked yourself *"Why would it have to mean that?"* and/or *"Do I still believe that?"* and have answered "no" you are on your way to feeling better. If you still feel that something is bothering you start over. You may have rushed yourself and perhaps you did not clarify enough *why* you are feeling bad. Remember that you have spent a lifetime acquiring and cultivating beliefs, which you never realized before, are actually contrary to the wisdom within you. The Option Method Questions will help you to uncover the beliefs that don't really serve you, the ones that seem to make you feel a way you would really rather not feel.

Review & Summarize

What am I unhappy about? (Identify)

What [is it] *about that*, that makes me unhappy? (Identify)

Why am I unhappy about that?

What am I afraid it would mean if I were not unhappy about that? *or*
What am I afraid would happen if I were not unhappy about that?

Why would it have to mean that [I don't care what I care about, for example]? *or*
Do I still believe that [being happy would be bad for me right now]?

Happiness Halting Beliefs

Here are just a few of the mythical beliefs that stop us from being happier:

* I cannot be happy unless _____ .
* I know I should but . . .
* I know I shouldn't but . . .
* You make me unhappy.
* I cause others to be unhappy.
* If I became content nothing would matter.
* I need _____ in order to be really happy.
* I'll be happy when _____ .
* If I were happy now it would mean I didn't care.
* If I were happy it would mean I didn't love them.
* I need people to love me.
* If I do _____ I will regret it (become unhappy).
* I know I'll be unhappy if _____ .

Did you ever notice that when you anticipate getting upset about something you begin immediately to feel upset? The moment we begin to fear or project that we will feel any way that we don't want to feel in the future we have already begun to feel that way in that very moment. It is likewise true of our good feelings. When we look forward to something happening it is almost as good as it happening! We immediately feel good and are in a good mood.

I believe that the most profound discovery that Bruce Di Marsico made through using the Option Method is that our current unhappiness is derived purely from our projections and imaginings of ourselves as unhappy in the future. More specifically, our *beliefs* about the future and especially the belief that something will make us unhappy in the future. The answer is not to become Pollyannas and convince ourselves that our futures will be bright, that all will work out. We know from experience that it doesn't always work out. The Option Method gives us a tool to use to question our beliefs and realize that whatever our future holds we don't have to feel unhappy about it. When we are free from these "future fears" as I like to call them, we will naturally be happier, kinder, more loving people.

Write down some of your happiness halting beliefs and future fears that you have uncovered while using this workbook. This list may serve you as a reminder that these are only *beliefs*, no matter how long you've held them, they are *merely* beliefs.

My Old Happiness Halting Beliefs & Future Fears

"You have within you the seeds for a beautiful garden. Spread them fearlessly."

— Bruce Di Marsico

What Causes Unhappiness?
by Bruce Di Marsico

The cause of unhappiness is a belief. What happens, no matter how undesirable or destructive to our life, health, desires or loves, does not cause unhappiness. The belief that we have to be unhappy is the only cause. To state it simply: if a person did not believe they had to be unhappy, they would not and could not be. We merely believe we need to have things or avoid things in order to avoid unhappiness.

1. Unhappiness is the feeling of a belief about a perceived or imagined phenomena; it is not an experience caused by the phenomena or anything else.

2. Unhappiness is experiencing your own believing that an event is bad and/or should not be because you believe IT causes unhappiness.

3. Believing something causes unhappiness is the very reason it seems to "cause" unhappiness.

4. Believing that something can cause unhappiness is the only cause of the fear of it. By "fear" is meant loathing, need to avoid, need to cure, need to kill or eliminate, disgust, hatred, terror, horror, repulsion, disdain and all such similar feelings.

5. Believing someone or something is morally wrong or evil, psychologically "sick," or behaviorally inappropriate is to fear that person or thing as if it could cause unhappiness.

6. Unhappiness is fearing that unhappiness can "happen" or be caused by anything.

7. Unhappiness is believing that something is necessary, something has to be, should be, ought to be, or must be other than what it is.

When a person is believing he/she has to be unhappy, what they are believing is that they have to be unhappy because they believe they are against themselves. The belief in unhappiness is the belief in being wrong for oneself. Unhappiness, in fact, means that I believe that I do, or want, or think, or feel a way that is bad for me.

A person believes: Certain things I do not want to happen may happen or are now happening. I don't want them to. I feel bad (and am worried or afraid now) because I "shouldn't" be thinking negatively about my life now. Maybe I should be wanting what is evidently happening anyway. I am denying reality, and that is wrong. I will be unhappy about this in the future because when certain things I do not want or do not like happen I will feel a way that is bad for me. It is wrong to expect misfortune. That is "unhappy" of me.

It doesn't matter whether the undesirable event happens to me from circumstances out of my control, or I think I am the cause or part of the cause; unhappiness comes because I believe that I now have proof that I am bad for myself.

"Bad for myself" means I am not really wanting for me what I "should" be wanting for me, and something can prove it. The belief is that this event "proves" it.

Basically, feeling bad means that I believe that what I do, or think, or want, or feel means I am against my own best interests. I believe that these are a bad way of doing thinking, wanting or feeling. The way I am being is a bad (wrong, self-defeating) way of being.

This could be called the same as believing that I will be a way I shouldn't be, or think a way I shouldn't or want or feel a way I shouldn't. If we didn't believe that we could be a way we "shouldn't" we couldn't feel unhappy no matter what else we felt.

All unhappiness is the fear that we have a bad attitude for ourselves. We are afraid that something proves we are bad for ourselves in the sense that we are in some way against what we are for, and for what we are against. We are afraid that we have a self-defeating attitude.

The fear that we have a bad, or self-defeating, attitude is the same as distrusting the very source or cause of our motivation. We are unhappy when we believe our very life, our heart, our self is against all that we live for; our personal happiness.

Happiness is the freedom to be as we are, however we are; richer or poorer, in sickness or in health, gaining or losing, succeeding or failing, wanting or not wanting, approving or not approving, forever. Happy is what we are and what we'll be if we don't believe we are wrong to be as we are.

The Creation of the Option Method
by Bruce Di Marsico

I created the Option Method for happiness. Sometime before 1970 I realized that people were unhappy because they "wanted" to be. They believed they "should" be. I knew that they believed it was good and necessary to be unhappy about whatever they believed that applied to, generally them not getting what they wanted. This was the way people chose unhappiness as a feeling.

Unhappiness is used here as a term or model word for all kinds of feelings that people describe variously as "bad" feelings. Feelings ranging from mild annoyance to murderous rage; from disappointment to suicidal depression.

The belief that unhappiness is preferable to happiness (happiness being seen as some form of being crazy), or the belief that not being unhappy was contradictory to a personally held value, is the dynamic of all unhappiness.

The belief goes like this: "If I wasn't unhappy about it, it would mean that I wanted it to happen." "If I wasn't sad (or angry, etc.), it would *mean* I didn't care."

All fear and unhappiness is the fear that unhappiness will happen.

I describe it like this: no person is afraid of being poor in itself but of being an unhappy poor person. No person is afraid of illness but of being ill *and* unhappy also. No one is afraid of a bear or of being hurt by the bear but of the unhappiness that they believe will occur from the hurt. The examples are countless but follow this paradigm. People are afraid unhappiness will "happen" to them under certain circumstances.

In order to reveal what beliefs are indeed operative in an unhappy person, I created the Option Method. This simple questioning method discloses to the sufferers that they are the determiner of their feelings. It shows that they are feeling exactly what they believe they should feel, always.

It just so happens, that when people realize they have a choice in their emotions, it makes a difference to them. People know they don't want to be unhappy when they don't believe it is necessary.

People feel now what they believe they are going to feel in the future. They feel whatever feelings they believe will "happen" to them. They feel now whatever they believe it will be "natural" to feel in the future, even if it is as a result of something happening now. The current event correlates to current emotions only insofar as it relates to imagined future feelings.

I created two questions as a simple demonstration of this phenomena.

"If you believed that at this time tomorrow you were going to be unhappy, what would you feel now?"

"If you were to believe now that at this time tomorrow you were going to become very happy, what would you feel now?"

The Option Method is not unlike the above, but its questions are more specific and personally applicable to the person being helped.

An important point to remember about my philosophy is that I do not believe that people should not be unhappy, or that they should be happy. The Option Method demonstrates that people choose their emotions, not that they should choose differently, but that they nevertheless truly choose, and are not victims to emotions. Admittedly, these unhappy emotions *seem* to happen to us. That is the unhappy quality of them that precisely makes them so mysterious, and therefore apparently necessary. They are meant to be feelings of helplessness, or we would not consider them unhappy feelings. That is the very fear that they manifest; helplessness, mystery, and need for control over our experiences in order to be happy.

It is apparent from the Option Method that what people need to be happy is the confidence that their happiness cannot be threatened, and therefore do not need to fear the helpless feeling that their happiness will be taken away.

Unhappiness is any form of believing that when we don't get what we want, it means we are going to feel a way we don't want. Unhappiness is also believing that if we get what we want, we will also feel a way we don't want.

Happiness is being glad for who you are;

* liking that you want what you want, liking that you don't like what you don't like,
* liking that you change your mind whenever you think that's best,
* liking that you don't change your mind until you really change your mind,
* liking that you don't like not knowing how to have what you want,
* liking that you don't like being mistaken,
* liking that you feel just the way you like to feel about everything you do, and
* liking that you feel just the way you like to feel about everything that happens.

Everything is the way it is, and you really can be glad to feel the way you do.

Bruce M. Di Marsico (1942–1995)

Portrait by Bruce Hancock

The creator of the Option Method, Bruce Di Marsico, originally studied to be a Catholic priest. Recognizing that what he was searching for was not within the confines of the seminary, Bruce began to find his true calling while studying psychology and philosophy in the 1960's at Seton Hall University, New Jersey. Years later, while working as a psychotherapist and human relations consultant, he came to develop the Option Method as a self-help tool for people to become happier in their everyday lives.

He introduced his method in New York City around 1970 at a paraprofessional school for group counseling and therapies called Group Relations Ongoing Workshops (GROW). Since then the Option Method has been taught to teachers, psychologists, therapists, social workers, clergy and other practitioners as an additional tool in their professions. Above all, Bruce created the Option Method to help people to help themselves to find their deepest wisdom and happiness.

"Bruce left an indelible impression on me. Time with him was mystical and transforming — his truths, a simple soothing balm. He could cut through a lifetime's worth of gnarled rooted anguish, and redefine what was and is, in a completely different way. I traveled through his eyes and his voice as he spoke ageless wisdom, guiding me through myself and changing me forever. Bruce was a powerful man with a profound gift." — JP

"Bruce Di Marsico taught me how to be happy. Before I knew him it was a chancy thing, an elusive experience that didn't happen often or last long. Every day I use his lessons to help me swim against the tide of belief in un-happiness in which we live." — Mandy Evans, author of *Emotional Options*

"Bruce's words are inspiring and I will keep them close to remind me of the source of my happiness and my choice to claim my right to perfect peace and joy!" — Geraldine Berbaum

"Bruce Di Marsico was devoted to teaching the truth that no one has to be unhappy in this world. He developed a method to help anyone who wanted to be happy see with new eyes. Bruce knew that the most profound love of another human being is acknowledging their freedom to choose their beliefs. His teaching changed my life and helped me build a rock-solid foundation on my life's journey to perfect happiness." — Wendy Dolber

Notes

Notes

Books and Tapes by Bruce Di Marsico

Unlock Your Happiness With Five Simple Questions: The Option Method
by Bruce Di Marsico • $11.95

During his lifetime Bruce's students frequently asked him to write a book. Bruce, it seemed, was much happier devoting his time to writing for his lectures and classes and spending time with his students. Whether he was sitting in his living room with them or around the kitchen table, Bruce preferred to teach in his own very unique dynamic way. He loved to be with students. He never did get around to publishing a book himself, but he left us with a wealth of material to work with.

In this book there is something for everyone, those who had the opportunity to know him and especially those who had not. *Unlock Your Happiness With Five Simple Questions: The Option Method* is the first book of his writings ever published. It encapsulates his entire philosophy and is based on material he developed near the end of his life. His widow, Deborah Mendel, has put together his most succinct work, writings that he had evolved and refined over the thirty years he shared Option with us. This book will not only help us individually to understand his Option Method and its principles, but provides a key tool in sharing Option with others. Whether exploring Option with friends or in ones own Option Method workshops or practice, this book is an invaluable guide.

The Option Method is not about memorizing questions. It's about understanding why you are asking them. In this book Bruce explains the philosophy behind his Option Method questions. Bruce explains how our beliefs affect our happiness. He describes the difference between wanting and needing. He sheds new light on the myriad forms our unhappiness can take while at the same time removing its mysteries. Finally he reveals how ". . . we cannot be bad for ourselves."

This compact book is simple, inspirational and challenging. Readers and students at all levels of Option study with have fun exploring Bruce's ideas in this book.

"Don't forget that you each personally bring something very special to Option. YOU! It's about the gifts you bring to the table. The moment you decide to help yourself or someone else using the Option Method, change has already begun. Trust." — Deborah Mendel

May be ordered from Deborah Mendel through *www.choosehappiness.net*, *www.optionmethod.com*, *Amazon.com* or send a check or money order for $11.95 (includes shipping) to: Deborah Mendel, P.O. Box 1192, Walnut Grove, CA 95690. Contact Deborah for quantity discounts.

The Key To A Happy Life
Bruce Di Marsico Presents The Option Method
35 minute audio CD • $12.50

This is the first recording of Bruce Di Marsico to be released. In this live recording originally taped in New York in April 1973, he shares his Method and the philosophy behind it. The timelessness of this lecture is breathtaking.

Discover the real Bruce Di Marsico; not fictional, not mysterious nor elusive, but rather a most kind and gentle man. Bruce explains in his own words how this simple self-help tool can free us from our self-imposed suffering to rediscover our personal wisdom and happiness. He demonstrates through stories and real life examples, how what we believe creates what we feel.

Bruce gently and clearly discusses his Option Method questions. He reveals how asking these questions can help us to uncover and let go of the judgments and beliefs that seem to stand in the way of our happiness. He continues to expand and explain the Method and how unhappiness only seems mysterious.

Learn why we use the Option Method,

". . . We look at ourselves because we don't like the way [our unhappiness] fits. We don't like the way our feelings fit us; they make us uncomfortable."

On "Why ask why?" Bruce says,

". . . We can't assume that everyone feels bad for the same reason . . . and we can't assume that about ourselves. We often do. We assume, 'Hey I'm unhappy for the obvious reasons.' What are the obvious reasons? The obvious reasons are sometimes not so obvious . . ."

Bruce teaches about unhappiness in personal terms,

". . . If I'm not going to see that some belief of mine is causing me to be unhappy, what's the first thing that happens? My finger starts to point . . . before you know it . . . we're blaming everything and everybody for our unhappiness, never looking at a belief that maybe we've outgrown, [a belief] that maybe doesn't fit anymore, [a belief] that maybe we don't need."

This audio CD may be ordered from Deborah Mendel through *www.choosehappiness.net*, *www.optionmethod.com*, *Amazon.com* or send a check or money order for $12.50 (includes shipping) to: Deborah Mendel, P.O. Box 1192, Walnut Grove, CA 95690. Contact Deborah for quantity discounts.

The Happiness Secret: Is Happiness a Choice?
The Option Method Philosophy
90 minute audio CD • $24.95

What role does choice play in our happiness or unhappiness? Do we indeed choose to be unhappy? This was the most common question asked by the Option students who gathered together at Bruce Di Marsico's home for this lecture recorded live in November of 1995, just a few weeks before he passed away. These fortunate students, most of who had studied at the Option Institute, had no idea that these would be Bruce's last recorded words.

Bruce clarifies what he means by "choice." He explains to his students how our beliefs affect our happiness and unhappiness. Bruce explores the connections between our feelings and our beliefs and just what kind of judgments cause us to feel bad.

Bruce describes how his Option Method works,

"[The Option Method takes unhappiness from] that vague cloud of confusion and that which just happens to you and brings it down to the real dynamics that cause your emotions . . . your beliefs and your judgments."

Bruce explains in this lecture,

". . . Unhappiness happens in the dark, it happens in the half light of reason. The problem is that you think you know that you have to be unhappy. I suggest that it's questionable. What if what you are feeling is just the result of a belief you have?"

Bruce discusses the purpose of the Option Method,

"Why are people afraid to be happy? This is the third question in the Option Method. What are you afraid of if you weren't unhappy about that? This [question] reveals the real reason [one has] for being unhappy."

In this lecture, his last before his death on December 4, 1995, Bruce shares with friends and students his kind understanding of human nature and happiness. Discover the root cause of your unhappiness through Bruce's profound insights.

This audio CD set may be ordered from Deborah Mendel through *www.choosehappiness.net*, *www.optionmethod.com*, *Amazon.com* or send a check or money order for $24.95 (includes shipping) to: Deborah Mendel, P.O. Box 1192, Walnut Grove, CA 95690. Contact Deborah for quantity discounts.

Books and Tapes by Mandy Evans
Emotional Options: A Handbook for Happiness
$11.95
Order from *Amazon.com* or call toll free 1-800-431-1579

In **Emotional Options** you will find a simple, step-by-step method to free yourself from beliefs you hold that affect your health and happiness — beliefs that limit your ability to love and be loved, beliefs that keep you from making healthy choices in life. Learn how to ask yourself the questions that will release your knowing. When you discover that what you believe is no longer true for you, you dissolve feelings of anger, fear, and doubt that have seemed inevitable — often for years. The result is happiness!

"It's beautiful. I finished it eager for more, much more!" — Bruce Di Marsico, founder of The Option Method

Travelling Free: How to Recover From the Past by Changing Your Beliefs
$14.00
Order from *Amazon.com* or call toll free 1-800-431-1579

"**Travelling Free** gives insight into freedom from victimization through outworn memories — to use your memories without allowing your memories to use you." — Deepak Chopra, MD, author of *The Seven Spiritual Laws of Success*

"A valuable tool for those seeking peace and direction." — Bernie Siegel, MD, author of *Love, Medicine and Miracles*

"**Travelling Free** bridges the gap between the psychological approach to wellness and the recovery model of 'twelve-step' programs. The simple, yet creative exercises can be done by anyone, anywhere." — *EastWest Journal*

"In **Travelling Free** counselor Mandy Evans addresses one of the most challenging issues of the recovery process: how to move from naming your pain to changing your beliefs and your life. Evans tells us that, if we want to change our lives, we need only turn, perhaps ever so slightly, and take the very next step in a new direction. It's never ever too late to change our course and create a new life." — *Body, Mind and Spirit Magazine*

"Mandy Evans' work with belief systems is strong and clear. She helps people overcome their self-defeating beliefs in an empowering way." — John Gray, author of *Men Are From Mars, Women Are From Venus*

Choosing Happiness
Audio Cassette • $10.00
To order call toll free 1-800-431-1579.

Includes actual dialogues recorded live at Interface. Funny, Insightful, Audacious!

Books by Frank Mosca, Ph.D.
Joywords: An Invitation to Happiness through
an Introduction to the Option Method
$11.95

Order from *Amazon.com* or *www.frank-mosca.com* or *www.frankmosca.net* or call 631-843-4115

Joywords is an introduction to the Option Method that utilizes both a step by step conceptual framework and actual edited dialogues with nine people who profited from this educational experience. You will find issues of panic attacks, sexual abuse, martial discord, failing health, loss of direction in life, breaking free from the constraints of the opinions of others, and fear of death. There are no limits to how happy you can become with this method, except the one's that you presently hold to be true. This work invites you to come to the fullest realization of your potential to live your life in joy.

The Option Method Joybuilding Workbook
$16.95

Order from *Amazon.com* or *www.frank-mosca.com* or *www.frankmosca.net* or call 631-843-4115

This book unravels the mysteries of how we get unhappy and shows you how to get past your specific problems and get more joy in your life, right now! It's literally a map through all the pain and suffering, the dead ends, the unwanted compromises, the broken relationships, and all the many disappointments that plague our lives. Step by step you are led through a re-education of your understanding about not only unhappiness, but also happiness. Joybuilding is filled with useful examples, exercises and detailed, down to earth instructions on how to use this breakthrough approach called the Option Method.

The Unbearable Wrongness of Being:
Exploring and Getting Beyond the Myth of Unhappiness
$13.95

Order from *Amazon.com* or *www.frank-mosca.com* or *www.frankmosca.net* or call 631-843-4115

The Unbearable Wrongness of Being is an exploration of the Option Method perspective through the device of literary vignettes taken from classic literature and altered to create an Option dialogue in each story. Join these fictional characters on a journey of discovery and find yourself opening the door to greater joy along with them!

The Godspeak:
A story of self-discovery
$14.95

Order from *Amazon.com* or *www.frank-mosca.com* or *www.frankmosca.net* or call 631-843-4115

A journey of self-discovery that includes spies, love, sex conspiracies. Follow Dan Ferino as he unravels a mystery that begins with a physicist's death. Join him in a chase across four continents against time as he seeks to save the world and more deeply to find meaning for himself. His discoveries will be yours as well; his self resolution will be a model for your own personal transformation.

Resources

"After my own writings, I turn to Frank Mosca's works as the best description of the Option Method."
— Bruce M. Di Marsico

"I have found your work outstanding. You have a real gift for effective metaphors and catchy phrases that I admire . . . I am so enthusiastic about your work . . . I consider your work profound, entrancing, and successfully offering a brilliant answer to one of the most urgent problems of our times: why are human beings so unhappy."—Ken Keyes, author and creator of the *Living Love Method*